The Quest

Volume 2 of "A Fervour of Bee"

Bhasrutha Reddy

Made with ❤ on the BookLeaf Publishing Platform
www.bookleafpub.in
www.bookleafpub.com

Dedication

To my beloved parents,

Thank you for your boundless blessings and unwavering support. Your encouragement has been the wind beneath my wings.

Thank you for inspiring me to reach for the stars and for always standing by my side. Your belief in me has been a constant source of strength.

To my family and friends,

Your endless love and hope have illuminated every step of my journey. Each of you has played a crucial role in this endeavor, and your support has made all the difference.

And to my dear Mom, Dad, and Brother,

You are the heart of this book. Your love and support have been the driving force behind my words and ideas. I am profoundly grateful for your presence in my life.

With all my love and gratitude,

-Bhasrutha Reddy

This book is dedicated to all who are courageously
pursuing their dreams and striving to
achieve their goals. Your relentless dedication and
passion are the inspiration behind this work.

  The Quest Volume 2 of "A Fervour of Bee" is a collection
of motivational poetry inspired by the
pursuit of your aspirations.

Here we dive into a realm of soul-stirring moments,
crafted to touch your heart and leave a
lasting impression.

May these words encourage you and remind you that
every step forward is a victory.

Pursuing dreams is a journey of courage and passion. It's
about chasing the whispers of your
heart, embracing uncertainty, and making aspirations a
reality. With each step, you move closer
to achieving the impossible. Believe in yourself and your
dreams, and never give up on making
them happen.

Life is often challenging, and sometimes events occur
that are beyond your control not your
fault. This doesn't signify failure but rather the need for
greater resilience. You must summon
your strength, persist through difficulties, keep pushing
forward and don't let setbacks defeat
you.

Preface

"A Reflective Spirit"
The little girl wept amid the uncertainty, her heart racing
as she broke down and sobbed through
the tunnel of chaos.
Her eyes are an ocean, vast and inscrutable, holding a
depth of hidden grief. Behind her smile
lies a mask that conceals the pain she endures, a hurt
that remains constant despite the shifting
tides of her emotions. Her laughter, though bright,
carries a subtle sadness, a reminder of the
deep sorrow beneath. Her gaze mirrors the ocean's
boundless beauty and wistfulness,
capturing a poignant blend of grace and heartache.

Emotions possess such a profound grip on the mind that,
despite one's efforts to forget, they
linger persistently in one's thoughts.
In the depths of our soul, thoughts stir our emotions, and
emotions flow into poetry, a symphony
of the heart.

Time moves on, yet we sometimes feel stuck. Turning
thoughts into actions can be challenging
because words often fall short. Manifesting is the process
of bringing our inner thoughts into
reality.

Learn to set boundaries that are stronger than your
empathy. Don't be so understanding that
you let everything slide. Be kind, but not naive. Protect
your peace.
"Some truths are too deep to be explained, only felt in
the silence of our own hearts."

Every journey unfolds as a tale of persistence and
passion. Though the path may be longer for
some, faith in the process and unwavering dedication
will ultimately lead you to your goals

Acknowledgements

Thank you for the amazing response and wonderful support to A Fervour of Bee Volume 1.

I'm excited to share **The Quest Volume 2 of "A Fervour of Bee"**. I hope you enjoy it as much as the first one.

I am deeply grateful to *Book Leaf Publishing* whose keen eye and dedication have helped bring this collection to life. Your expertise has been instrumental in shaping these poems into their final form.

To my readers, thank you for allowing my words to touch your hearts and for embracing the emotions woven into each poem.
Your connection to my work gives it life, and it is your empathy, and support that inspire me to continue crafting these verses.
This book is for those who turn to poetry in search of solace, joy, or understanding. These poems are as much yours as they are mine. I hope the words within these pages find their way into your heart, offering comfort, reflection, or simply a moment of connection. Thank you for walking this path with me.

1

SUCCESS OR FAILURE

The desire to achieve is strong enough to overcome any
obstacle. Despite the ups and downs,
it serves as a shelter in the storm, a comforting touch, a
source of courage, and a way to dry
your tears. This strength has to build self-belief, and you
must be committed to persevering, no
matter what you need to persist with unwavering
determination.
You spend your days urging others not to give up, even
as you grapple with your own
uncertainty about how to move forward.
Do not blame yourself for things you are not accountable
for. Sometimes, circumstances may
not be in your favor but regret is not the only solution.
Challenges are opportunities for growth.
Rather than fearing failure, focus on pushing through
and conquering the stairs towards
success.

Keep trying. You have the ability to overcome obstacles.
Persevere and do not give up. Stay resilient.

WIN OR LOSE?

WIN OR LOSE?
"When you are exhausted, what does your mind think?
Why does your stride falter in the pursuit
of life's goals?"
"I will assure your tearful eyes of victory, gently wiping
away their sorrow. I will nurture the hope
that I will live up to your trust. And I will promise your
joy that there are no bounds to its delight.

Even if you lose it all,
And trust is broken by the fall,
While breath remains and spirit's flame,
No force can dim your destined aim.

Though the world may turn its back,
And shadows cloak your chosen track,
Hard work will forge a path to rise,
Guided by relentless skies.

Honesty will call success your way,
And discipline will clear the fray,
With each step steadfast, sure, and free,
Victory's yours, as it's meant to be.

2

A Mercy Tale

Is suffering a choice or simply fate?
In the journey of life, we seem to encounter it repeatedly.
Each beat of the heart bears the
weight of an overwhelming agony that has accumulated
over time.
Once upon a time, there was a girl deeply worn and
drained by her emotional struggles. The
mounting stress had woven itself into a tapestry of
trauma. Exhausted and overwhelmed, she
would cry out in her moments of despair.
One day, amidst her suffering, she spoke to her mother
about her illness. Her mother, holding
her close, offered words of solace: "I know it's hard, but
everything requires patience. Stay
strong; time has a way of healing."
The girl remained silent, deeply mystified. She wondered:
Does endurance have a limit? Why
does it feel so unfair? She sought a resolution for her
forbearance, yearning for at least a
moment of peace from the misery in her life.

3

Inner Turmoil

When the internal struggle begins, conflict, uncertainty,
and bewilderment converge within the
mind. we can articulate a few thoughts, few we can
listen to, some we can observe, and a few
we can let go.

Yet, there are certain things we hold in our minds. It is
not wrong to endure suffering. Each tear
we shed comes from the heart, and Every thought we
have holds a depth of significance.

Breath may be one, but our emotions are endless.
Feelings are countless.

Sometimes, it's fine to wear a smile so bright,
While beneath, the shadows stir in the night.
You might seem calm as life drifts along,
But darkness circles, a haunting song.
You tell yourself all is well and clear,
Yet tears fall softly, betraying your fear.

You may shatter, drained and cold,
Emotion and loss in a grip so bold.

The struggle, the tears, the pain—it's all yours,
A web of sorrow where despair endures.
May your fleeting joy end on a sweet note,
Not in a decade of sorrow that chokes your throat.
Trauma presses hard, a heavy chest,
The pain recurs, never letting you rest.
Echoes stab, suppressing every tiny sting,
As your heart cries out, fear taking wing.

Amidst it all, a deep sadness grows,
A profound ache that nobody knows.

4

THE GLEAM OF STRENGTH

Somewhere in the darkness there is a shadow like a ray of bright power.
Be Optimistic.

Say to yourself.

Dear self,
I love you for growing stronger each day.
If life were a book, my favorite chapter would be healing.
Every page has shaped who I am today.
Your lessons were like happy tears, helping me find my smile.
Thank you for always bringing hope for tomorrow.
Trust your worth and abilities, and have faith in your journey.

You alone hold the power to save yourself, and your
strength is worth every effort. The battle
may be fierce and invisible to others, but the greatest
triumph is when you rise resiliently, true to
your destined self.

5

THE DEEPEST CORE OF INTROSPECTION

A full stop is not the end; it marks the moment where
new beginnings emerge after the dot.
Silence is not finality; it is a hidden realm of unspoken
depths, brimming with endless
possibilities.

The biggest plight is being disconcert in the beginning,
uncertainty in between dumbstruck in the
end.
We learn from the times we are hurt and understand our
worth through the times we suffer.
We are mere pawns in the intricate game of life. Success
and failure are just part of it.

We often perceive these moments as divine tests,
uncertain whether they are unsure whether
they signify fortune or misfortune.
As time distances us from our experiences, memories
tend to blur.
It is prudent to confront challenges early, before they
grow into more significant issues.

6

A Tranquil Gaze

Embrace the power of growth by burying your
inhibitions and embracing what is meant to
elevate you.
While the world seems to be in a rush, Like the wind
blows, feel the caress of Breath.
Like the ocean flows, heal from the depth.
Evolve around Ignite the blaze of your intellectuality.

In the vast garden of life, I stand beneath a sky painted
with dreams so grand With every step, a
seed of growth I sow Burying inhibitions deep below
Unshackling fear, I spread graceful wings embracing
challenges that learning brings for in each
struggle lies a hidden door Leading to the treasures I so
adore.

Let go of doubts, let loose the mind's reign For
possibilities shall break every chain with open
heart, I welcome what will come embracing weaknesses,
strength will blossom
through trials and storms, I shall not falter for they are
but steps on my path to alter rising
above, I'll reach for greater heights embracing growth,
embracing pure delights
So let inhibitions be buried deep within.
Embrace the power that lies beneath our skin For in
embracing what elevates our soul
We'll conquer mountains, reaching our true goal.

7

A constructive advice to Balance

It's up to you to choose happiness or sadness. Work on
restraining impatience and embrace
your identity. Love and admire yourself for who you are.
Think positive.

At the end of the day, the major thing is who you are
and what you stand for.
Your strength and stability come from within.
Embrace your enthusiastic spirit.
Be the dominant and predominant version of yourself.

Choose yourself with intense desire.
Smile at the incredible strides you take.
Be your own source of inspiration.

8

Life's Lessons: Growing with Integrity

The lessons we learn in school are numerous, but life itself is a far greater teacher. Every step we take should be guided by these lessons. A person's future hinges on their commitment to their chosen path. Despite the challenges, when we reflect on our character and values, our decisions should bolster our self-confidence and honor. Mistakes should not lead to self-doubt or shame. Instead, they should serve as opportunities for growth, allowing us to maintain our dignity and integrity.

Just because you refuse to give up doesn't mean the
journey is easy. Often, the fiercest battles
are fought in the quiet depths of our struggles, where no
one can see the toll they take. But it's
in that silence where true strength is forged, and when
victory finally comes, it shines all the
brighter for having been won in the shadows.

9

Evolving

Maybe this is what they mean by healing and how time changes things. It's strange. Take a
moment to look at yourself and understand.

In life, you may think you dislike compromising, yet you've compromised and moved on more
than you realize. Turn back and reflect.

Sometimes, we try to escape certain situations, and when nothing works out, we get used to
them and learn to adjust. Knowing ourselves, taking space, understanding things with a clear
mind, and going with the flow is what growth is about. That's how you prove yourself.

HARMONY

Do you ever feel overwhelmed by your own empathy, as
if it's pulling you in countless
directions? It's easy to become entangled in the desire to
help and please everyone around you.
But here's the reality:
While empathy is a profound and admirable quality, it
can sometimes blur the line between
kindness and self-neglect. We must cultivate boundaries
that are as strong as our compassion.
Setting these boundaries isn't a sign of unkindness; it's a
mark of wisdom and self-respect. It
means recognizing when to say "no" to protect your own
energy and well-being. By doing so,
you're not just safeguarding yourself, you're also
teaching others how to respect your limits.
Remember, you can offer grace and kindness without
losing yourself in the process. Prioritize
your own needs, uphold your values, and protect your
peace with confidence.

10

A Reflection on Life

In life, one of the greatest mistakes people often make is foolishness. It might seem trivial, but
it's profound. As they say, anger is one's enemy, and foolish actions taken in arrogance can lead
to significant harm.
This behavior might appear minor in our daily lives, but when viewed from a broader
perspective, considering both the past and future, the damage becomes evident. It's crucial to
make changes before small habits escalate into major problems. Misunderstandings with
parents, friends, or anyone can stem from differences in opinions or thoughts.

Ignoring some things is okay, but disregarding good advice, regardless of the source, can lead
to significant loss. We should cultivate good habits and follow the right path. Mistakes should be
the responsibility of those who make them.

Everyone should strive for good habits and a proper
approach to life. Our parents and friends
who care for us always try to guide us. Ignoring their
advice and stubbornly making mistakes
can lead to greater troubles later on.
Listening to good advice can prevent unnecessary
arguments and regrets. If we end up alone
with our mistakes, we risk losing the respect and trust of
those who care for us. Realizing our
mistakes too late will only lead to regret.
It's better to learn and correct ourselves while we still
can. Thinking ahead and acting wisely
ensures that our journey goes as planned, whether today,
tomorrow, or later. There's no rush,
but never stop trying. This is the essence of growth,
proving yourself through continuous
self-improvement and thoughtful actions.

11

Your triumph lies within your grasp

he chasm between speaking the truth, concealing it,
maintaining silence, and lying is as vast
as the distance between earth and sky. When trust is
genuine, anyone can articulate anything,
whether to close family or strangers. Yet, countless
emotions remain unspoken, deeply rooted
within.

Recognizing these nuances is vital, though fools, driven
by arrogance, often miss the point.
They see nothing beyond the path of criticism. In places
devoid of trust, even a thousand
reasons are like blowing a conch into deaf ears. Such
individuals are like impenetrable walls.
There's no need to justify yourself to every tree along the
path. Those who truly know you will
understand the expanse of your heart and the emotions
behind your silence without requiring an
explanation.

In time, the depth of these emotions will reveal itself.
That moment isn't just any ordinary time, it
is your victory, your triumph. You must forge that
moment yourself. When the world looks at you
with admiration, your enemies, witnessing your success,
will be silenced in their envy and
regret. Their silence becomes your triumph.
With joy and strength, fused with integrity, you can
ascend to any height without hesitation.

12

Everything That Happens Is for Our Good

Sometimes, when life doesn't unfold as we wish, time
offers us a unique opportunity—the path
illuminated by the divine. This path, more harmonious
than any other, is the one truly worth
following.

No matter how uncertain or disorienting the present
road may seem, as long as we tread with
unwavering faith, integrity, and courage, these virtues
will lead us forward.

Even when courage wanes, time itself will provide
clarity and answers. In the face of adversity, if
all you have is time, rely on it. Your resilience will
eventually reveal a way forward. Your
experiences will open doors to new worlds and new
wisdom.

13

An anguished writing

I scribbled in a desperate mood.
I endured in a devastated feels of my tiny heart scrutiny,
Vanishing the needs of sorrow and agony,
The sense of disappearance might wreck my misery.
Perhaps, it's the only recourse to run away from injury.

Life is an Evolution.

"Some truths are too deep to be explained, only felt in
the silence of our own hearts."
Change is an essential part of growth, shaping us into
who we are meant to become. It
challenges our comfort zones, pushing us to adapt and
evolve.
By embracing change, we discover our strengths and
move forward, allowing us to reach our
full potential.

Peace emerges when you recognize that what lies
beyond your control should also be beyond
your mind. Letting go of these concerns clears the way
for inner calm and serenity.
Like butterflies that pause in the rain to shield their
delicate wings, it's essential to allow yourself
rest during life's storms.
When the storm passes, you'll find your strength and be
ready to soar again.
You'll be astonished at the opportunities that unfold
once you truly believe in your own worth."

14

The Silent Ascent: Victory Through Unspoken Trials

In an untold story, many words remain unspoken, and
countless lessons lie beyond the surface
of a mature personality. At first, aspiration arises from
despair, propelling you to climb the stairs
toward your goals, one step at a time.
Persisting through challenges doesn't mean the journey
is easy. Often, the most intense
struggles occur in the silence of darkness, and it is
through these trials that the light of victory
eventually shines brightest.

15

The True Measure of Worth: Understanding and Self-Awareness

Your worth is apparent to those who truly understand
you, and it is enough for your mind to
remain at peace. Those who know you will grasp the
essence of your character, even if you
remain silent. Conversely, those who do not understand
you may never fully appreciate what
you have to offer, no matter how much you explain.

It is not necessary to seek validation from everyone; the
key is to recognize and value your own
capabilities. If you are aware of your own strengths, you
possess the power to overcome any
challenge.

Remember, true success is always an ascent.
Keep this in mind.

16

The Power of Belief: Navigating Faith, Effort, and Self-Confidence

In today's world, atheism is increasingly common. However, this discussion isn't meant to dismiss theism but to highlight a point of reason. When we ponder the existence of God, the essence of belief remains central. Regardless of one's stance, a belief system is crucial in life. Even a small amount of faith can provide substantial trust. For example, when faced with a minor health issue, we seek medical help because we trust in its efficacy. This trust stems from our belief in the reliability of medical professionals, guiding our actions with a firm conviction.

Similarly, if we believe in a higher power, that belief
shapes our perspective and actions. It's a
fundamental driving force. The presence of belief—
whether in a deity or in oneself—manifests
in our actions and attitudes.
Assuming that divine presence guarantees success or
that its absence results in failure is
misguided. Success and failure hinge on our efforts and
perseverance. When things don't go as
planned, it may simply mean that greater opportunities
are on the horizon. Even if progress
seems slow, new chances may emerge.
Fate and luck certainly play roles, but the true keys to
overcoming challenges are self-belief and
confidence. Embrace a positive outlook, and remember
that anything is possible. Each belief
reinforces the conviction that you can achieve your
goals.

17

The Journey Within

In life, each heart yearns to attain some grand prize,
Yet along this path, many trials arise.
Joy or sorrow? Hardship or delight?
Through all these tests, we must persist and fight.
At times, while running, you may tire and pause,
But rise without faltering, adhering to the cause.
For he who continues shall reach the goal,
And find the joy of success enriching his soul.
When victory is won, the pleasure so profound,
Yet laziness may tempt you, causing you to be down.
The pain of regret surpasses hard work's strain,
The heart's deep wounds, unseen, endure the most pain.

Let your heart weep till it has shed its tears,

For what hurts today will soften with years.

The wounds on your body may heal with time,

But the scars on your heart are vast and sublime.

Desire goodness and seek what is right,

Your thoughts shape the path through the night.

Never cease striving, let not your effort wane,

Wipe your tears and rise again.

Search for joy, keep running in grace,

Whether success or failure you face.

Within your soul, find your satisfaction,

Start your journey anew, guided by your own direction.

.

Decide whether happiness or sorrow will reign,

For you are the master of your own domain.

18

"Patience Is Key"

Achieving anything in life is never easy. You must
navigate through ups and downs as you
progress forward. On this journey, each step may bring
challenges that seem overwhelming, but
strive to rise above them for your growth. Obstacles are
tests of your perseverance.

Despite the delicate nature of your heart, "Learn to
approach some difficulties with more ease."
Do not be disheartened by setbacks, my friend.
Significant changes may lie ahead in your
destiny—embrace them as opportunities for growth.

Remain unwavering in your pursuit, and let your focus
remain fixed on your goal.

19

Resilience

Hey, listen, take a breath, you've got this—
In a realm of fear, the way may seem tough.
It's fine if healing's still underway,
Surviving through a rigid tragedy's play.
This year may have thrust you into doubt,
But I know you're trying, striving without a doubt.
While battling for yourself, thoughts may linger,
Just accept where you are; let hope be your singer.
You'll conquer this, let it inspire your quest,
Be kind and true to yourself, give it your best.
Forgive the past, let the younger self fade,
Grow with grace, let new paths be laid.
Embrace your inner child, but don't be ensnared
By haunting paradoxes that leave you impaired.
Hold strong aspirations, build your own way,
Even in darkness, let your effort light the day.

20

Veiled

In every life, a hidden fight,
Behind the smile, the shadows lie,
A facade that masks the deepened plight,
While true emotions silently cry.

The world may see a cheerful face,
Yet hearts endure a secret strain,
What's visible is but a trace,
Of inner battles, hidden pain.

To judge or scorn without the view,
Of all that's felt and all that's known,
Is to miss the struggles true,
And cast unjust stones, alone.

21

Fortitude

Though the path is steep and long,
And battles fought in silence strong,
Where shadows hold the fiercest fight,
Strength is born out of the night.

When the world can't see your pain,
And struggle seems to be in vain,
Remember, strength is what you gain,
Through every tear, through every strain.

The journey's tough, the road is long,
But in your heart, the will is strong.
And when you rise, where you belong,
Your victory will be your song.

What if everything you're enduring is actually setting
you up for the things you've longed for?
Each struggle might be shaping you for the fulfillment of
what you've always desired.

Eventually, you will discover the answers you seek. In
the meantime, embrace the present, trust
your choices, and have faith in yourself. You're exactly
where you're meant to be right now.

Your vibration is a unique signature that resonates with
the universe. Elevate it through positive
thoughts and actions, and you'll attract the same
uplifting energies into your life.

THE END.

Concluding this volume with a lovely smile.

~BHASRUTHA REDDY